A HANDBOOK OF
CATHOLIC POLITICAL PHILOSOPHY

A HANDBOOK
of
CATHOLIC
Political Philosophy

BASED ON THE ENCYCLICALS OF LEO XIII

GERALD C. TREACY, S.J.

Imprimi Potest:
FRANCIS A. MCQUADE, S.J.,
Provincial.

Nihil Obstat:
JOHN M. A. FEARNS, S.T.D.,
Censor Librorum.

Imprimatur:
✠ FRANCIS CARDINAL SPELLMAN,
Archbishop of New York.
New York, October 7, 1947.

XIII Books
An Imprint of Arouca Press
Waterloo, ON N2J 0A5
www.aroucapress.com

ISBN: 978-1-998492-71-8

CONTENTS

POPE LEO XIII

MARCH 2, 1810: Born at Carpineto
in the Papal States.

1818–1819: Student at Jesuit College, Viterbo.

1824: Roman College, Academy
of Ecclesiastical Nobles.

1832: University of the Sapienza.

DECEMBER 31, 1837: Ordained Priest.

FEBRUARY, 1838: Apostolic Delegate, Benevento.

1841: Apostolic Delegate, Perugia.

1843: Nuncio to Belgium. Archbishop
of Damiata (Titular).

1846: Bishop of Perugia.

1853: Cardinal.

FEBRUARY 20, 1878: Pope.

JULY 20, 1903: Death. "I do not know how men
will judge me, but I know I have always
greatly loved the Church and have tried
to procure her good. So I die tranquil."

A Modern Pope in a Modern World

VINCENT JOACHIM PECCI became Leo XIII on February 20, 1878. Pius IX had died on the 7th of February. The Conclave had been short. The new Pope was elected on the third ballot. He was a frail man in his late sixties. He was born in 1810 at Carpineto in the Papal States.

When his election was announced he exclaimed: "I am a feeble old man. I cannot bear so great a burden. In a few days I shall collapse. Death and not the papal dignity will be mine." The Romans hoped that he would survive his coronation. He did and for a quarter of a century ruled the Church.

Leo XIII was the first modern Pope for he approached the problems of the modern age as none of his predecessors had done. From the time of the French Revolution which gave birth to the modern world, the Popes had condemned every modern error as it appeared. And they did so fearlessly. Leo XIII would do this, too, as was his duty. For he was Christ's Vicar. But he would not rest satisfied with condemnation. He would not only patiently unmask error, but he would meet it by forcefully teaching truth.

Leo XIII showed his technique in his first encyclical *Inscrutabili*. This was issued April 21, 1878. After pointing out the evils of the age, the Pope began by declaring that civilization could not save itself without the Church, as the Church had always been the greatest force for civilization in the world. This note was to recur again and again during the twenty-five years of his pontificate. It is that "the Church of Christ far from being alien to or neglectful of progress, is its nurse, mistress and mother." He declared that there can be no true civilization unless it rested on virtue, truth and justice.

And not only the Church but the Roman Pontiffs in particular have ever played the role of protectors of civilization down through the centuries. "It is truly the glory of the Supreme Pontiffs that they have ever placed themselves steadfastly as a wall and bulwark to save human society from falling back into its former super-stition and barbarism." Since the Papacy has been the source of so much good to mankind, the Pope owes it to mankind to preserve and uphold the dignity of the Papacy. So he pledges himself to strive for three objects: That his authority may receive due recognition; that all obstacles that hamper its free exercise may be removed; that his civil sovereignty may be restored to him, since it is necessary for the protection and preservation of his full liberty of action as a Spiritual Ruler. He urges the leaders of the nations "for their own peace and safety as well as for the peace and safety of their peoples, to mitigate the evils that are assailing the Church and its Head."

The social order was upset, Leo XIII declared, because men had rejected the basic truths on which a healthy social order must rest. For men chafed under authority and set themselves against it in all its forms. This would lead to revolution and war. There was a widespread contempt for law, there was a mad rush for riches, and waste, theft and even treason stained the records of many high-ranking public servants.

The Pope then calls upon the children of the Church to deepen their love of their Faith and their loyalty to the Holy See; to realize the supreme importance of Catholic education and to do all in their power to widen the respect due to God's Law especially in regard to marriage and the family.

This was Leo's inaugural statement to the world. Eight months later he issued his first encyclical *Quod Apostolici Muneris*. This

encyclical discussed three philosophies that
were taking shape in political action: Socialism, Communism, and Nihilism. Because
these philosophies have penetrated political life, many governments are godless, civil
authority is regarded as something of merely
human origin, and Christ's teaching has been
banished from education. There is a bitter
struggle everywhere between the many and
the few, the *haves* and the *have-nots*. Belief
in a future life is fast disappearing from the
minds of men. That is why the many are seeking for opportunities to plunder. The few are
living in constant fear; fear for their lives and
their possessions.

The revolutionary movements of the
day, Socialism, Communism, and Nihilism,
threaten the three basic principles on which
civilization is built; the divine origin of
authority, marriage and the family, and the
right of private property. These movements
have their origin in the teaching of the sixteenth century innovators who not only broke

with the Church, but brought about the rejection of Revelation, the subversion of the supernatural order, and the enthronement of reason as man's only guide for living. This was the Rationalism of 1878 that had permeated all civilized society.

In 1881 Europe was stunned by the assassination of Alexander II of Russia. This occurred on March 13th, and Nihilists were proved guilty of the murder. It was the beginning of a long series of assassinations or attempted assassinations of Russian officials that ended only with the collapse of the Romanoffs.

Leo XIII on June 29, 1881, with the memory of Alexander's murder still fresh in the minds of men, issued his encyclical *Diuturnum Illud*, his first treatise on political philosophy. It treats of State authority and civic obedience. A few years later, on November 1, 1885, he issued *Immortale Dei*, on the right Catholic attitude toward the modern State. On June 20, 1888, he gave to the world the encyclical on

Human Liberty, *Libertas Praestantissimum*, and on January 10, 1890, the encyclical *Sapientiae Christianae*, on the Civic Duties of Catholics. As *Rerum Novarum* and *Quadragesimo Anno* give us the Christian Social Philosophy, so do the above-mentioned encyclicals give us the Christian Political Philosophy.

CHAPTER I

State Authority and Civic Obedience

Diuturnum Illud

WHAT IS A POLITICAL PHILOSOPHY?

It is a set of principles governing political life. It deals with the rights and duties of rulers and subjects.

WHAT IS THE FIRST PRINCIPLE OF CHRISTIAN POLITICAL PHILOSOPHY?

Authority is necessary. The State cannot exist without it. Obedience to this authority is the duty of citizens.

WHAT IS THIS AUTHORITY CALLED?

Government.

IS STATE AUTHORITY REVERENCED TODAY?

No. Ever since the sixteenth century the prestige of State authority has diminished. In the sixteenth century private judgment was pitted against Church authority. In the passing years the result has been a weakening of respect for *all* authority.

WHAT ARE THE MODERN FALSE THEORIES ON STATE AUTHORITY?

Individual liberty is an unlimited right; all authority in the State derives exclusively from the people; the ruler is nothing more than a delegate of the people; at the people's whim the ruler's authority may be withdrawn.

WHAT IS THE TEACHING OF THE CHURCH ON AUTHORITY?

All authority comes from God. The ruler may be selected by the people. Such selection points out the ruler, designates the ruler. It does not confer on him the right to rule. The people do not hand over authority; they *determine* by whom authority shall be exercised (*Diuturnum Illud*).

DOES THE CHURCH ADVOCATE ANY SPECIAL FORM OF GOVERNMENT?

No. The Church approves any just form of government that secures the common welfare, is suited to the needs of the people and expresses their will.

ON WHAT IS THIS TEACHING BASED?

On Sacred Scripture and the Fathers of the Church, notably St. Augustine, St. John Chrysostom, and St. Gregory the Great. No theory of civil authority is more in keeping with reason or more profitable to the welfare of rulers and people.

3

HOW IS AUTHORITY RELATED TO MAN'S LIFE IN SOCIETY?

First, it is according to man's nature to live in society. It is as natural for man to live in society as it is for a bird to fly. As God is the Author of man's nature, He is the Author of society. He created that nature. Society needs rulers. For there must be a depositary of power to direct the wills of the members of society toward the common good. That there should be rulers therefore is God's Will.

WHAT IS OF PRIME IMPORTANCE TO THE RULER?

It is of prime importance that the ruler should be able to enforce obedience so completely that disobedience to the command is *sinful*. But no man has this within his own power, as this belongs to God alone, the universal Creator and Lawmaker. It follows then that those who exercise this power exercise it as something communicated to them by God. And this holds for every type of authority.

4

The Origin of Society

WHAT IS THE MODERN AND FALSE IDEA OF THE ORIGIN OF SOCIETY?

Society arises from the common consent of its different members, and authority has the same origin. Each one by an agreement surrenders part of his rights, and freely puts himself under the power of some person to whom the sum of these rights is given.

WHAT IS WRONG IN THIS THEORY?

It ignores the fact that man is social by his very nature. Because he is a man he has the urge to live in society. Moreover this agreement theory is a pure invention. It could never give to political authority that degree of force and prestige which is necessary for safeguarding the State and the common good. Authority will only possess all the dignity and safeguards it needs, if it is realized as something coming from God, the most sublime and holy of all sources.

HOW DOES THE CHRISTIAN TEACHING ON AUTHORITY AFFECT THE RULER AND THE CITIZEN?

It enhances the prestige of the ruler. If authority comes to the ruler from God it is worthwhile and more than merely human. Because citizens in giving loyalty to their ruler are giving loyalty to God. They submit out of *reverence* for authority and not from fear of punishment. They act from a spirit of duty and not of adulation. Rebellion is far from their thoughts or they realize that to resist lawful State authority is to resist God. Whoever refuses respect to the ruler refuses respect to God.

HOW DOES THIS TEACHING STABILIZE GOVERNMENT?

It safeguards justice for rulers realize that authority is given them not for personal profit but for the good of the people. They are aware that their rule must resemble God's rule from Whom they receive their power to rule. They are conscious that their rule must be carried out with justice and faith, and that when severity is needed it must be tempered by fatherly love. If they betray their trust they know that they cannot escape God's judgment (*Diuturnum Illud*).

HOW DOES THIS TEACHING AFFECT THE CITIZEN?

It upholds his dignity as a man. For in obeying he loses nothing of his worth as a human person. He realizes that before God there is no distinction of persons, there is neither slave nor free, there is but one Lord of all. He obeys his ruler because in his ruler he sees a reflection of God, to serve Whom is to reign.

THEN IT IS NEVER RIGHT TO DISOBEY STATE AUTHORITY?

Yes it is. When State authority commands anything that openly conflicts with the Natural Law or God's Law. For in that event the

State is overstepping the limits of authority and perverting justice. Where there is no justice there is no duty.

HAS THIS TEACHING SHOWN ANY PRACTICAL RESULTS?

Yes, even from the days of Pagan Rome. Persecution could not shake the loyalty of the early Christians to the State. Nor did it deter them from service in the army. But when they were commanded to do what was sinful, they preferred to leave the army and face death rather than to rebel against the State.

DID THE CHURCH CARRY ON THIS TEACHING AFTER ROME BECAME CHRISTIAN?

Yes. She insisted that the Christian Emperors should regard their authority as something sacred. Hence the custom arose of anointing the new ruler. That is why the institution of the Holy Roman Empire came about.

WHAT HAVE THE MODERN THEORIES OF THE STATE AND AUTHORITY ACCOMPLISHED?

They have brought confusion and bitterness to rulers and peoples. For to refuse to acknowledge God as the Author of authority is to strip authority of its strength and glory. If the people are the *only* source of authority, its foundation is fragile and unstable. The consequence will inevitably be disorder and rebellion.

HOW DID NIHILISM, SOCIALISM, AND COMMUNISM ORIGINATE?

They originated in the false teaching of the sixteenth century innovators who rejected the divine authority of the Church. Rebellion, especially in Germany, followed fast upon these teachings. Then came the false philosophy of the eighteenth century in France teaching the New Jurisprudence and advocating unlimited liberty for the individual. These are the sources of Nihilism, Socialism, and Communism.

WILL PENAL LAWS ENFORCE CIVIC OBEDIENCE?

Penal laws alone will not and cannot. For as St. Thomas points out, fear is a weak foundation for civic obedience. For those who are subdued by fear will more readily revolt once the chance presents itself. Fear drives men to desperation which provokes new revolts.

WHAT IS THE REAL SUPPORT OF CIVIC OBEDIENCE?

Religion. For loyal obedience to the authority of the State arises from a sense of duty and filial fear of God. It is Religion that inculcates this obedience and develops it. For Religion affects the *minds* and *wills* of men. It not only disposes them to obedience but unites them to their rulers in bonds of friendship. Religion is the best guarantee of public peace.

WHAT SHOULD THE STATE'S ATTITUDE BE TOWARD THE HOLY SEE?

For the safety of the State itself rulers should defend Religion and grant full liberty of action to the Church and the Holy See. For the State owes much to the Holy See, as the Popes have always checked religious revolutionaries, and have warned the people and their rulers against these men as enemies of society itself.

WHAT IS THE TEACHING OF THE CHURCH ON CIVIL GOVERNMENT?

The Church teaches that civil affairs belong exclusively to the State. Matters that are partly civil and partly religious should be peacefully adjusted by concordats between Church and State. The Church teaches rulers to govern with justice and upholds their rule. Ever the friend of freedom and the foe of tyranny, the Church tempers human harshness, making laws more equitable and customs more humane. It is always God Who gives to rulers salvation and to their peoples the beauty of peace.

CHAPTER II

The Catholic Citizen in the Modern State

Immortale Dei

WHAT IS THE OPENING NOTE IN THE ENCYCLICAL "IMMORTALE DEI"?

A note that Leo XIII sounded again and again during his pontificate. He insisted that the Church was the mother of civilization, the friend of progress, and ever in sympathy with all the aims of government. Although the Church's mission is primarily the salvation of souls, yet the temporal good she does for men is so extensive that it might appear that man's earthly welfare were her main concern.

WHAT DOES "IMMORTALE DEI" PORTRAY?

The Christian State. This State acknowledges God as the Source of authority, and the Model for the exercise of that authority. It professes its duty to God and Religion; it honors and protects the Church. It stays within its own sphere and does not invade the sphere of the Church, but co-operates with the Church in all matters that concern the welfare of the citizen. It honors God by the public profession of Religion for it admits that society no less than individuals owes a debt of gratitude to God.

WHAT IS THE ATTITUDE OF THE CHRISTIAN STATE TO THE CHURCH?

It acknowledges the Church's independence in everything that pertains to the religious life of the citizen. Whatever belongs to the salvation of souls and the worship of God belongs to the jurisdiction of the Church. Whatever pertains to the civil order is subject to the jurisdiction of the State.

WHAT OF MATTERS THAT PERTAIN TO BOTH CHURCH AND STATE SUCH AS EDUCATION?

There should be co-operation and co-ordination between Church and State. There need be no conflict over the respective rights of each.

HOW DOES THE CHRISTIAN STATE REGARD THE CIVIL SOVEREIGNTY OF THE POPE?

It admits that the Holy See needs civil sovereignty as the best safeguard of its independence.

15

ON WHAT IS THE CHRISTIAN STATE FOUNDED?

On the principles of Christian philosophy, and it is governed by the same.

WHAT FOLLOWS FROM THIS?

Laws are made for the common good. They are framed by truth and justice and not by caprice. Rulers are obeyed because they hold their authority from God and exercise it in His Name. Citizens in giving obedience to their rulers know that they are giving obedience to God. Obedience is not the service of man to man but submission to God's Will expressed through the medium of men.

HOW DOES THE MODERN STATE COMPARE WITH THE CHRISTIAN STATE?

It is in direct contrast with the Christian State. It claims that all sovereignty resides entirely in the people and so all authority derives exclusively from the people. It holds that unlimited freedom of thought and speech is a natural right. It places the Church on a plane with all other societies and makes it subject to the State. It calls this separation of Church and State. It considers all religions equally true and good, and pronounces this toleration.

WHEN DID THE MODERN STATE ARISE?

It really began in the religious revolt of the sixteenth century which produced confusion in Religion, philosophy, and in the social order. It reached its full stature in the French Revolution of 1789.

WHAT THEORY CAME OUT OF THIS REVOLUTION?

The New Jurisprudence which is at variance with the Natural Law and traditional Christian teaching.

WHAT ARE ITS MAIN PRINCIPLES?

1. All men are equal by nature and race; so they are equal in the control of their lives.

2. Each person is master of himself and in no sense under the rule of any other individual.

3. Each person is free to think as he likes and to do as he pleases, so no man has the right to rule over another.

4. Government is the rule of the people. It is a delegated administrator for the people; the people is its own ruler.

HOW DOES THE MODERN STATE REGARD RELIGION?

With indifference as Religion is a matter of private judgment. As the State is a multitude which is its own ruler it owes no duty to God. It grants equal rights to all creeds for the sake of public peace and order.

HOW DOES THE MODERN STATE VIEW THE CHURCH?

It looks on the Church as a private association like any other association. It denies the Church's divine foundation and mission. It claims the right to appropriate Church property, denying the Church the right to hold property. In matters that are of interest to Church and State, it ignores the Church. For example it legislates on marriage without considering the Church. In the eyes of the State, the Church has no legal rights. Her corporate life continues only by favor of the State.

DOES THE CHURCH PREFER
ANY SPECIAL FORM OF GOVERNMENT?

No. The Church approves every form of government that is just; that is built on the consent of the governed; that aims at procuring the common good.

HOW DOES THE CHURCH VIEW
SCIENTIFIC PROGRESS?

With approval. The Church recognizes in truths discovered by science a reflection of the Divine Intelligence. It has never disapproved the true scientific improvements of the times.

WHAT SHOULD BE THE CATHOLIC CITIZENS' ATTITUDE TOWARD THE MODERN STATE?

While disapproving of the principles held by many modern States, the Catholic citizen should be active in civil life. He should be interested in local and national politics. Otherwise, political life will be controlled by those whose principles will find expression in laws and policies against the common good.

WHAT IS THE CHALLENGE TO THE CATHOLIC CITIZEN?

He must never compromise with false principles but combat them with all the power of truth. Catholicism cannot come to terms with Naturalism or Rationalism whose aim is to sterilize Christianity, exclude God from Society, and make man a law unto himself.

CHAPTER III
True Liberty

Libertas Praestantissimum

WHAT IS LIBERTY?

It is the power of choice rooted in man's soul.

WHAT IS THE FOUNDATION OF LIBERTY?

The foundation of liberty is in the fact that man's soul is immortal, endowed with reason, and immaterial. This has been the constant teaching of the Church. Never has she compromised with fatalism.

HOW MAY THE POWER OF CHOICE BE FURTHER EXPLAINED?

It is the power of selecting suitable means for the end a man has in view. He judges this thing is good and chooses it.

HOW DOES A MAN'S SOUL DIFFER FROM HIS BODY?

Man's body is of the earth, earthy; man's soul is simple, that is without parts; it is spiritual, that is immaterial or non-earthy; it is intellectual, that is capable of reasoning.

DOES MAN ALWAYS CHOOSE WHAT IS GOOD IN USING HIS LIBERTY?

No. He always chooses what *seems* to him to be good. The defect of liberty is in this fact that man may choose what is *really* bad because he *judges* it to be good. The power to choose what is bad is a proof of liberty and also a proof of its imperfection.

WHAT IS LIBERTY'S BEST SAFEGUARD?

Law. As liberty is imperfect it needs guidance. This guidance comes from Law. For Law is a rule directing what is to be done and what is not to be done. The guidance of Law and its sanctions help toward a right choice.

HOW MAY LAW BE DIVIDED?

Law means God's Law and human laws.

WHAT IS GOD'S LAW CALLED?

The Eternal Law and the Natural Law. The Natural Law is the Eternal Reason of God the Creator and Ruler of the world, implanted in reasoning creatures and inclining them to their right action and end. It is our reason bidding us do right and avoid wrong. As God has given us a destiny, the Natural Law points us toward that destiny.

IS THE NATURAL LAW THE SAME AS THE ETERNAL LAW?

Yes. It is the Eternal Law active in reasoning creatures. The commands of reason have the force of law only in so far as they interpret a Higher Reason. Unless it agrees with the Natural and Eternal Law no human law has any binding force.

HAVE WE ANY OTHER HELP TO THE RIGHT USE OF LIBERTY?

Yes. God has given us Grace. This gift sheds light into the intellect and pours power into the will. It does not impede liberty but works with it, making its use easier and safer.

WHAT IS THE LIBERTY OF THE CITIZEN?

Freedom under law. As a citizen man is associated with others in society and the field of his liberty is marked out by law. Some laws express the Natural Law. Others follow indirectly from the Natural Law and decide many points which the Natural Law touches only in a general way. These laws give a particular rule of life; they are detailed applications of some principle of the Natural Law.

IN WHAT DOES TRUE LIBERTY CONSIST?

In the rule of law and not in the freedom of all to do what they please. In obeying human laws we lead our lives more easily in conformity with the Eternal Law. As human laws have their origin in the Eternal Law and conform to it they oblige us in conscience to their observance.

DOES HUMAN LAW OBLIGE ONLY SUBJECTS?

No. It also obliges the ruler. The liberty of the ruler does not mean the power to command unreasonably or capriciously. An unreasonable law has no binding force.

WHAT DOES TRUE LIBERTY ALWAYS IMPLY?

It implies the obligation of obedience to a supreme Eternal Law, that is to the authority of God.

WHAT HAS BEEN THE EFFECT OF THE CHURCH'S TEACHING ON AUTHORITY?

Obedience to law is ennobled, for it is really obedience to God. It safeguards the rights and interests of all, restraining excesses on the part of the ruler as well as the subject. Mutual duties as well as rights belong to both.

WHAT IS LIBERALISM'S TEACHING ON LIBERTY?

Extreme Liberalism teaches that man is a law unto himself as there is no divine authority. Authority in the State comes from the collective will of the people. Whatever the majority wills is right. Rights and duties have their source in the majority-will.

Reason is the supreme judge; good and evil are merely matters of opinion; whatever pleases the people is lawful. Law is what the majority wills and its final power rests on physical force.

WHAT DOES MODERATE LIBERALISM TEACH?

Moderate Liberalism teaches that man should be guided by the Eternal Law but only as it is known by reason. God's revealed truth is discarded.

WHY IS THIS FALSE?

Because man is obliged to take his standard of life not only from the Eternal Law but from all other laws that God has made known through Revelation.

IS THERE ANOTHER TYPE OF LIBERALISM?

Yes. There is a type of Liberalism that acknowledges the force of the Eternal Law in private life but denies that it has any bearing on the political life of the State. Religion and morality are divorced from the life of the State so that in framing civil laws, God's Law may be ignored.

WHAT DOES THIS GENERALLY MEAN?

The subjection of the Church to the State under the name of separation of Church and State.

WHAT SHOULD BE THE RELATION BETWEEN CHURCH AND STATE?

Both should work together for the common good. In some spheres they are separate, and in others they meet, as in the field of education.

HOW MAY THE ENCYCLICAL ON TRUE LIBERTY BE SUMMARIZED?

1. There is no such thing as unconditional freedom of thought, speech and worship compatible with true liberty.

2. A just reason warrants freedom in these matters and it is not unconditional but moderate freedom.

3. Whenever the people are oppressed or the Church deprived of liberty of action it is lawful to work for a change in government.

4. It is lawful to prefer a democratic form of government based on the true teaching on the origin and exercise of authority.

5. Catholic citizens should take an active part in local and national political life.

6. Every State is entitled to self-government and freedom from any foreign despotic power. Governments should promote the greatest amount of prosperity for their citizens.

CHAPTER IV

Catholics' Civic Duties

Sapientiae Christianae

HOW DID LEO XIII CHARACTERIZE THE WORLD OF 1890?

Disorder was prevalent everywhere, and there was general neglect of Christian teaching.

WHY DID MODERN STATES FEEL INSECURE?

Because their only reliance was on force, and force is more apt to beget slavery rather than loyalty. What was needed was the revival of Christian Religion in the family and in every sector of civil society.

WHAT IS THE CATHOLIC CITIZEN'S TWOFOLD LOYALTY?

Loyalty to God and to Country. There need be no conflict of loyalties. Loyalty to God means loyalty to the Church. Both loyalties stem from the same eternal principle. God made both Church and State. Conflict comes from the State ignoring God's Law and invading the rights of the Church.

IF SUCH A CONFLICT ARISES WHAT IS THE DUTY OF THE CITIZEN?

He should obey God rather than men, as the Apostles taught in the first days of Christianity. Laws contravening God's Law are not laws at all.

WHAT THEN IS LAW?

A mandate of right reason promulgated by properly constituted authority for the common good. A command at variance with truth and divine reason cannot be in accord with human reason. No authority is properly constituted unless it is founded on God's Law and proceeds from God.

WHY IS OBEDIENCE DUE PROPERLY CONSTITUTED AUTHORITY?

Because it is a symbol of the Majesty of God. Obedience to this authority proceeds from a consciousness of duty, not from fear of force or threat of penalty. Laws at variance with the Eternal Law, the teaching of the Church or of Christ's Vicar are to be resisted. To obey them is a crime.

WHAT IS AN ESSENTIAL DUTY OF THE CATHOLIC CITIZEN?

To love both Church and Nation. This is the essential duty of all Catholics and the source from which all their other duties arise.

WHAT IS THE DUTY OF CATHOLICS WHEN NATURALISM'S TEACHINGS ARE ADOPTED BY THE STATE?

To keep the Faith burning brightly in their own hearts. In the face of modern false teaching every Catholic should show forth the Faith that is in him, proclaim it fearlessly, and encourage his fellow Catholics to do the same.

WHAT ARE THESE MODERN ERRORS?

Disbelief in God and Divine Revelation; rejection of the Church; proclaiming Nature as the source of truth and the code of human conduct.

HOW DO THESE ERRORS FIND EXPRESSION?

Often in State laws that aim at the weakening of Catholic life, encouraging elements hostile to the Church, adopting measures demoralizing to the people.

CAN CATHOLIC INACTIVITY BE DEFENDED IN THIS SITUATION?

No. To remain inactive is cowardly and insulting to God. There is nothing more encouraging to the wicked than cowardice on the part of the good. In the battle against error the zealous Catholic citizen has God's assurance of success.

IS THE TEACHING APOSTOLATE OF THE CHURCH COMMITTED TO THE LAITY?

Yes. While it is primarily the office of Pope and Bishops it is also the duty of the laity for all are called to share in the task of giving to others what they have themselves received. The Vatican Council declared that as far as possible the zeal of the laity should be enlisted in spreading Christian truth and warding off error.

WHAT SPIRIT MUST PERMEATE THIS APOSTOLATE?

The spirit of unity. For Christ founded His Church as a single body, His Mystical Body. As one single organism it must give battle. It is one army set in battle array and no single individual is free to select his own mode of fighting. He scatters and gathers not, who gathers not with the Church and with Christ. Those who do not battle in this way of unity, in fact battle against God.

DOES THIS MEAN MORE THAN UNITY OF ACTION?

Yes. It first means unity of *minds*. And this implies not only perfect accord in one Faith but complete submission to the Church and to Christ's Vicar as to God Himself.

IS THIS SUBMISSION ONLY DUE TO THE POPE?

It is due to the Pope and the Bishops whom the Holy Spirit has appointed to teach and rule over the members of Christ's Mystical Body.

HOW DO CHURCH AND STATE DIFFER IN THEIR SPHERES OF ACTION?

The Church is a society established by God to lead men to holiness and peace. She has fixed laws and a spiritual field of action. The State is founded to secure the temporal welfare of men.

MAY THE STATE SHARE IN THE SPIRITUAL AUTHORITY OF THE CHURCH?

No. It was not to Caesar but to Peter that Jesus Christ entrusted the keys of the Kingdom of Heaven.

DOES CHRIST'S KINGDOM RESEMBLE EARTHLY KINGDOMS OR STATES?

In a way it does for its authority is exercised through laws and institutions. But in its origin, in the principles of its nature and its life, the Kingdom of Christ differs completely from all other kingdoms or States.

WHY IS THE CHURCH CALLED A PERFECT SOCIETY?

Because it has within itself every means to achieve the purpose for which Christ founded it. It needs no human power for the success of its mission. It is superior to all other societies because it is divine in its purpose and in the means with which our Lord has endowed it to secure that purpose.

SHOULD CATHOLIC CITIZENS FOLLOW ONE SPECIAL POLITICAL PARTY?

No. In political questions there is scope for difference of opinion among Catholics. Nor should anyone strive to drag the Church into party strife. When the interests of Religion and the Church are at stake all political differences should cease among Catholics and all should present a united front.

IS THE CHURCH INDIFFERENT TO THE POLITICAL LIFE OF THE STATE?

No. For it is the duty of the Church to see that Christian ideals pervade the life of the State. It is also her duty to oppose any law that exceeds the State's competence and invades the rights of Religion.

WHAT SHOULD THE STATE PROCURE FOR THE CITIZEN?

The opportunity to earn a decent living and to develop his mental and spiritual powers. The duty of the State is to so safeguard man's temporal welfare that he may the better secure his eternal destiny.

DID LEO XIII HOLD CATHOLIC CITIZENS RESPONSIBLE FOR THE BAD POLITICAL SITUATION?

He said that they were largely to blame for their inertness and for the dissensions that prevailed among them. Had they lived closer to their Faith and the standard of morality that it teaches, things would not have come to such a pass.

WHAT DID THE POPE SAY WAS THE WRONG CATHOLIC ATTITUDE?

The attitude of false prudence and timidity. It was expressed by those who abstained from attacking false opinions for fear of exasperating minds already hostile. Such an attitude was cowardly. It was the equivalent of fighting on the side of the enemies of truth.

CAN INDIVIDUAL CATHOLIC ACTIVITY PROMOTE THE CAUSE OF TRUTH?

No. Unless Catholic activity is united and disciplined by the Christian virtues it will avail little. Those individuals who reject the guidance of the Pope and the Bishops, preferring their own opinions, really damage the cause of Christ.

WHAT WAS LEO XIII MAINLY CONCERNED ABOUT?

He feared for the Nations of the world as they were losing their Christian heritage. He pointed to history to prove that sin reduces nations to slavery. He said that this age would not escape God's just judgment and that there were signs already pointing to the coming of world catastrophe.

WHAT IS THE CRYING NEED OF SOCIETY?

A return to truly Christian life. The foundation of that life is charity. Without it all other virtues are sterile.

WHAT ARE SOME PARTICULAR NEEDS OF SOCIETY?

Society particularly needs a better family life, for the wellbeing of the State rests on the family. Parents must realize their responsibilities and resist any State interference with their God-given rights. They owe their children a Christian education. The foundation of the State is the Christian home.

The Story of the Encyclicals

hen Leo XIII became Pope, the world was in the throes of revolution. In his first encyclical *Quod Apostolici Muneris*, the Pope drew a picture of Europe in 1878. The revolutionary theories of Nihilism, Socialism, and Communism were rife. They expressed themselves through political parties. As a result of their activities godlessness had penetrated the governments of Europe. Civil authority was declared to be of human origin, and Christ and His teaching were banished from political life.

A fierce struggle was going on between the many and few. The few had too much wealth, and the many too little. The few were living in constant fear. The many were seeking for opportunities to plunder the few. For years the Popes had warned governments against these theories that were at the root of the unrest of 1878. But governments welcomed their own enemies rather than accept the teaching of the Church.

The revolutionary movements of the day threatened the three basic principles on which civilization rests: the divine origin of authority, marriage and the family, and the right of private property. The revolutionists aimed at uprooting the foundations of civilized society. They attacked the idea that obedience to properly constituted authority was a duty, and maintained the absolute equality of all men in respect to their rights and duties.

Quod Apostolici Muneris exposed the errors of modern Rationalism, Nihilism, Socialism, and Communism. It was a summary of modern errors and their refutation based on the traditional teaching of the Church. It was the beginning of the series of great encyclicals that were to follow, giving to the muddled world a complete social and political philosophy.

Three years later when Europe was stunned by the assassination of Alexander II of Russia, Leo XIII issued *Diuturnum Illud*. The Pope took the occasion of the Emperor's assassination to remind the nations that the war so long waged against the Church had become a war against society and the rulers of States particularly. To meet this threat to civilization it was the paramount duty of rulers and subjects to acknowledge the rule of God over human society and conform their policies and their lives to that rule.

Immortale Dei was issued on November 1, 1885. It was an analysis of the Modern State and a directive to Catholic citizens on their attitude toward the Modern State. As the Modern State was built on the false teachings of the French Revolution as contained in the Declaration of the Rights of Man, issued by the National Assembly, Catholics were in a quandary. What were they to do? Were they to strive to find a working policy with the Modern State? Were they to separate themselves from all political activity? Or were they to strive to overthrow these false principles by political action?

Nowhere was this problem more pressing than in France. In 1885 France was a republic, the Third Republic controlled by an aggressive anti-Catholic clique. France had gone through five revolutions in fifty-five years. In the lifetime of Leo XIII France had been an empire under Napoleon, a kingdom under the Bourbons, a kingdom again under the citizen-king Louis Phillipe, a republic once more, then an empire under Napoleon III, and finally in 1885 a republic for the third time.

Judged by electoral returns the Third Republic was popular with the French people.

Yet since 1879 it was hostile to the Catholic Religion and growing more so day by day. Leo XIII felt it his duty to save French Catholicism in a republic that was opposed by leading French Catholics.

French Catholicism was divided in political outlook. There were monarchists, imperialists, and a small group of republicans. All were at odds with the Third Republic and at odds with each other. It was the desire of some to destroy the Third Republic for political reasons and of others to destroy it for religious reasons. There was also a moderate party, quite numerous, trying to work out a way of life under the Third Republic while completely rejecting its philosophy. Their plan was to live their citizenship to the full and by using their rights to bring Christian principles to bear on legislation.

Their fellow Catholics of the other groups denounced these moderates as bad Catholics. Controversy grew bitter involving the whole Catholic body, clergy as well as laity.

And while Catholic controversy raged the anti-Catholic regime kept steadily on its way.

Leo XIII made an exhaustive study of the French problem and after hearing the leaders of the different groups gave his answer in *Immortale Dei*. That answer was not only a guide for French Catholics, it was a directive for all Catholics living under governments whose constitutions rested on anti-Christian principles. It showed the Catholic citizen how to exercise his citizenship without compromising his Faith.

Nearly every country in the world was faced with the problems that *Immortale Dei* was intended to solve, but they were more acute in France than elsewhere. The monarchist party did not receive the encyclical favorably. Even Bishops and priests began to instruct the Pope, and journalists with monarchist sympathies interpreted *Immortale Dei* in a way that discredited the republican regime. Bitter controversy continued. Leo XIII through his Nuncio in Paris tried to reconcile the irreconcilables. After two and a half years, the Pope made it still more clear in an encyclical that Catholics could be loyal citizens of the Modern State, and that they should take an active part in its political life. On June 20, 1888, he issued *Libertas Praestantissimum*, on Human Liberty. This was followed a year and a half later by an encyclical that warned Catholics not to wait until the Modern State had become Christian before taking part in its political life. That policy spelled disaster. *Sapientiae Christianae* was published on January 10, 1890.

This completed the Pope's treatise on political philosophy. The following year *Rerum Novarum* appeared. It contained the principles of Christian Social Philosophy which Pius XI was to reassert and apply to the changed economic and social world forty years later in *Quadragesimo Anno*.

49

XIII Books is dedicated to publishing new and vintage works centered around politics, the economy, and the family. Named after Pope Leo XIII—the pope of the "working man," whose pontificate was the first to comprehensively engage in the Church's relationship with the modern world—our imprint was born out of the conviction that we cannot separate the Catholic faith from our involvement with the world around us, and that the social doctrine of the Church, whether explicitly or implicitly, requires a commitment by Catholics to transform every aspect of the social order in conformity to the will of God. We aspire to earn a reputation amongst our readers as a reliable provider of the best the social tradition has to offer, which is rooted in our allegiance to Christ the King and passion for sharing with others the teachings of the Church.